BE YOUR OWN
heroine

BE YOUR OWN
heroine
LIFE LESSONS FROM LITERATURE

sophie and charlotte andrews

illustrated by yelena bryksenkova

CICO BOOKS
LONDON NEW YORK

To Mum and Dad, for always supporting their daughters in whatever they wanted to do. And also to my sister and co-author, Charlotte. Your little sister may have beaten you to getting her name on a book cover, but I would never have been able to do this second book without you.

Published in 2020 by CICO Books
An imprint of Ryland Peters & Small Ltd
20–21 Jockey's Fields   341 E 116th St
London WC1R 4BW   New York, NY 10029

www.rylandpeters.com

10 9 8 7 6 5 4 3 2 1

Text © Sophie Andrews and Charlotte Andrews 2020
Illustrations © Yelena Bryksenkova 2020
Design © CICO Books 2020

Designer: Emily Breen
Art director: Sally Powell
Head of production: Patricia Harrington
Publishing manager: Penny Craig
Publisher: Cindy Richards

A CIP catalog record for this book is available from the Library of Congress and the British Library.

ISBN: 978-1-78249-896-4

Printed in China

CONTENTS

introduction

In 2018, the process of writing my first book, *Be More Jane*, allowed me to explore interesting life lessons in Jane Austen's novels and letters, and proved to me that her characters and social commentary remain relatable and relevant to this day. It also struck me that Jane Austen was a trailblazer: all her novels have strong and realistic female protagonists at their heart, which was such an innovative portrayal of women for literature at that time. Austen and other early female novelists, such as the Brontë sisters, Mary Shelley, and Elizabeth Gaskell, paved the way for the literary heroine to shine and flourish.

Inspired by Austen's leading ladies, I began to think about other famous literary heroines. Can we learn from great female characters in our other favorite books? Can we even become our own heroine by taking lessons from their stories? "An interesting starting point for another little book," I thought; so it was exciting to discover that my lovely publishers had been thinking along similar lines.

While I do of course love books by a huge variety of authors and of different genres, from historical fiction to crime, comedy, fantasy, and more, it is fair to say that my absolute forte is all things Austen! So I decided it would be fun to research and write this next installment alongside my older sister, Charlotte.

Allow me to introduce her: Charlotte is almost five years my senior, and she and I grew up together, attended the same schools and shared many interests, especially music. In fact, we are still to be heard playing piano and clarinet duets from time to time and love a joint theater, concert, or cinema trip! But it might surprise you to learn that Charlotte was always the avid bookworm in our family. I remember she would fill a small suitcase with books to take on our family holidays, and somehow she managed to read every single one. In fact, she even had a go at writing her own "novels," which were scribbled in notebooks and kept under her bed. I only caught the reading bug in my teenage years, and it was all thanks to Jane Austen: I fell in love with the 2005 movie of *Pride and Prejudice* and was thrilled when we later had to read and study the book at school: the rest, as they say, is history...

After an enjoyable few months of reading, talking, and writing together, over numerous mugs of hot chocolate, we are now excited to present to you some of our favorite female literary heroines, and what we have learned from them.

First, what do we mean by a literary "heroine"? Being the main female character is not enough in itself, so what elevates them to this esteemed state and inspires our respect and admiration? We thought about this and concluded that a heroine is someone who displays and promotes good moral values, and aims to love, thrive, and protect others, even when it is challenging to do so. To understand what makes our chosen characters heroines, we need to explore both their social interactions and their internal thoughts and moral compass. Mindful and considerate words and actions, unconditional love and loyalty: these are certainly conspicuous qualities among our favorites, which shape their relationships with family, friends, romantic partners, enemies, and even themselves!

From the endless library of wonderful novels that we all know and love and from the thousands of inspiring characters written by authors over hundreds of years, it has been almost impossible to choose just six key female literary figures for our little review, but after much soul-searching Charlotte and I have managed it and, rather nervously, we now present them to you. We are really hoping, with fingers crossed, that you approve of our final selection. Do please forgive us if we have missed out your own particular favorite—maybe next time?

Of course, we just couldn't write a book on heroines without including my blog persona, Elizabeth Bennet from *Pride and Prejudice*. Published at the start of the nineteenth century, this is the earliest novel in our selection and offers us an insight into women in society during that era. Austen was a clever and humorous observer of personality and behavior and as human nature doesn't really change, her depictions still seem totally believable and relevant today, so Lizzy Bennet is our first choice.

Our second heroine of classic literature is Jo March from *Little Women*. Louisa May Alcott's semi-autobiographical novel was published in 1868–69, about fifty years after *Pride and Prejudice*, and is set in the USA, so it gives us a different perspective on family life and young women. It is an authentic "coming-of-age" tale, as well as a romance, and has always been a much-loved bestseller. It still attracts an audience of younger and older fans today, so including Jo March was another absolute must.

Our next choice is July from the highly acclaimed novel *The Long Song* by Andrea Levy. The story is once again set in the nineteenth century, but the book was written and published in 2010. Levy tells the story of July, born a slave on a Jamaican sugar plantation in the early 1800s. She is a complete contrast to our other heroines so far: not only is she written from a historical rather than a contemporary perspective, but her life experiences differ vastly from our other two nineteenth-century heroines. July struck a real chord with us—it's possible that July is a new character for some of you and if so, we hope that you will feel inspired to delve into her story more deeply.

The same goes for our next heroine, the title character of *Eleanor Oliphant is Completely Fine*. If you haven't yet discovered this more recently published gem by Gail Honeyman, we hope that you will be inspired to read it. Despite her loneliness and troubled past, Eleanor's tale has an uplifting ending and she is a truly worthy heroine. Spoiler alert: the novel has such a clever twist in its tale that you might prefer to read the novel first, as inevitably we have had to give a few things away. Eleanor is such a remarkable and original personality that we really warmed to her and had to include her in our top six.

For our final two heroines, we decided to escape into the world of fantasy. We chose an inspiring young activist as our next heroine, Katniss Everdeen, from the hugely popular trilogy *The Hunger Games* by Suzanne Collins, published 2008–10. *The Hunger Games* books have sold in their millions worldwide and were made into globally successful movies. Since they are set in a dystopian universe, Katniss' life experiences provide an interesting contrast to those of our other heroines.

You can probably guess our sixth and final choice of heroine—a real favorite of Charlotte's from childhood right through to adulthood, and from the best-selling books of all time. Of course, she's Hermione Granger from J. K. Rowling's worldwide phenomenon that is the *Harry Potter* series. You could say that Charlotte grew up in parallel to Hermione, waiting on tenterhooks for the next installment, and devouring each new novel as soon it was published. She and Hermione were even about the same age when each new book appeared. I doubt Hermione will need much introduction, but suffice to say that despite the "magical" setting of the stories, she is a credible and lovable character, written with warmth and a good amount of humor. We have really enjoyed the opportunity to include her in our little book of heroines.

our leading ladies

LIZZY BENNET

HER STORY In Jane Austen's world-renowned novel *Pride and Prejudice*, our spirited and witty heroine Elizabeth Bennet is one of five daughters, whose mother desires nothing but to see them all suitably married and financially secure. When wealthy Mr. Bingley rents a house nearby, Mrs. Bennet immediately pinpoints him as a potential future husband for one of her girls. However Lizzy unknowingly catches the eye of Bingley's friend, the rich landowner Mr. Darcy. Darcy's outward air of arrogance and superiority causes Lizzy to feel initial dislike, which is compounded by false stories of his bad character, as reported to her by the handsome scoundrel Mr. Wickham. Further insulted by his low opinion of her family, Lizzy refuses Darcy's proposal of marriage, but later receives his letter of explanation, which exposes Wickham's lies. Elizabeth regrets her hasty judgment and her opinion begins to change.

The couple meet again, accidentally, when Lizzy visits his incredible Derbyshire estate with her aunt and uncle, but the shock news of her youngest sister Lydia's elopement with Mr. Wickham causes a now lovelorn Elizabeth to return home to support her family. When it comes to light that Darcy has been secretly active in resolving the Bennet family's problems, Lizzy's love grows deeper, but after the family scandal, she believes all hope is gone. However, misplaced pride and unfounded prejudice is finally overcome and the story ends with a double wedding, not only of Lizzy with Mr. Darcy, but also her sister Jane and Mr. Bingley, much to the delight of Mrs. Bennet!

STRENGTHS Throughout the novel, Lizzy refuses to conform to the expectations and pressures of early nineteenth-century society. She is independent, intelligent, and well-read, and so self-assured that she is never afraid to speak her mind. She has chosen the path of true love over wealth, going so far as to refuse marriage proposals that would have provided financial security for herself and her family.

"I am only resolved to act in that manner, which will, in my own opinion, constitute my happiness, without reference to you, or to any person so wholly unconnected with me."

A LITTLE DEEPER Lizzy is not easily swayed by the opinions of others—on the contrary, she is exceptionally self-confident in her own judgments. However, this inclines her to be blinded by prejudice, a failing which she admits of herself toward the end of the story.

MEMORABLE MOMENT Lizzy cannot believe she finds herself in a farcical proposal scene with her ridiculous cousin, the clergyman Mr. Collins, who fails to take no for an answer! Not only that, but her mother threatens never to speak to her again if she refuses his offer of marriage. Fortunately, her sensible father discloses that he will never see her again if she accepts.

JO MARCH

HER STORY Louisa May Alcott's classic novel *Little Women* tells the story of Jo March and her three sisters, Meg, Amy, and Beth, and their passage from childhood into womanhood in mid-nineteenth-century Massachusetts. Jo is an avid reader and writer, often to be found composing romantic stories in the loft. Through work and play, Jo and her sisters enjoy carefree, fun, and educational younger years, alongside their neighbor Laurie. When she matures, Jo faces new challenges and decisions as she searches for her purpose in life. With Meg happily married, Amy exploring society in Europe, and Beth frail after scarlet fever, the sisters are moving in very different directions. Jo pursues a career as an author, and while living in New York as a governess she befriends Mr. Bhaer, an intelligent and caring professor.

Young adulthood is no easy ride for Jo: she endures a deep, painful guilt that she cannot return Laurie's romantic love, then crushing disappointment when her beloved novel receives scathing criticism, and raw heartache at the loss of her dearest sister Beth. But eventually, she finds her true calling. She and Mr. Bhaer recognize the love that has evolved from their friendship and they marry. When they establish a boarding school, Jo finds fulfillment in educating the boys in her care.

STRENGTHS Jo is a true force of nature. Intelligent, proud, and self-aware, she knows her own mind and does not allow others to influence her thoughts, words, or actions. She resolutely follows a path shaped by her own dreams and desires, not one dictated by the opinions of family or the expectations of society. It is a path of uncertainty and even failure at times, but it leads her to a wonderfully fulfilling destination.

A LITTLE DEEPER Jo is guided by her heart and seems to experience more passionate emotions than her sisters. Her fiery temper ignites treacherous flames on frequent occasions during her childhood, however she can equally fall into an artistic broodiness and retreat into herself.

This intensity also fosters fierce loyalty to her sister Beth during her illness. Jo rushes home from New York to nurse Beth, barely leaving her post by the sick bed. After Beth's death, she mourns for her sister deeply, for a very long time.

"Every few weeks she would shut herself up in her room, put on her scribbling suit, and fall into a vortex, as she expressed it, writing away at her novel with all her heart and soul, for till that was finished she could find no peace."

MEMORABLE MOMENT Jo stubbornly spends one entire morning making a mockery of the social convention of "calling" on friends and family. For her own secret amusement, she dresses inappropriately, introduces unsuitable topics of conversation, and even goes off to play with the children and a muddy dog! By the end of the morning, Amy is truly despairing of her sister's unladylike comportment!

JULY

In Andrea Levy's historical novel *The Long Song*, July is enslaved on a sugar plantation in early nineteenth-century Jamaica. Conceived when the plantation overseer rapes her mother, she is callously separated from her mother at the age of eight by Caroline, sister of the plantation owner. She is stripped of her identity: Caroline insists upon calling her new handmaid Marguerite, because "July is not a suitable name." She grows up knowing only a life of servitude, yet continually straining against the bonds of passive obedience that her mistress tries to beat into her. July makes the best of her lowly status, along with the other houseslaves—her surrogate family—by covertly making fun and fools of their masters.

However, July's surprisingly happy little world is ripped apart when rumors of emancipation spark violent uprisings and equally brutal retaliation by the plantation owners. July loses friends and family in the ensuing bloodshed as slavery officially ends, although the transition period proves equally turbulent. In practice, her position as handmaid to Caroline changes very little—until, that is, Robert Goodwin arrives on the scene as the new overseer. A passionate but short-lived romance with Goodwin sees July elevated above her fellow servants, and she even experiences an extremely satisfying superiority over Caroline for the first time in her life. But when Goodwin and Caroline abandon July and the plantation to return to England, July's life takes another dramatic turn and she must suffer extreme hardship, hunger, and poverty. A final twist sees July reunited with her long-lost son and living out her final years at peace, writing her memoirs.

STRENGTHS July is unswervingly positive and endearingly cheeky throughout, in spite of the chaos and violence of the times she lives through. It is sass and optimism that sees her successfully survive the horrors and live to enjoy a contented old age.

A LITTLE DEEPER With Goodwin's infatuation, July finds herself in an unfamiliar position of authority. However, her thoughtless words, poor decisions, and regrettable actions during this time are not what we might expect of a heroine. She flaunts her romance with Goodwin in front of a miserable Caroline and loses the respect of her friends by assisting Goodwin. But perhaps we can forgive her? July's life has never been her own to steer. Everything has been dictated by others and therefore she has no experience to draw upon in her sudden rise in status. It is only by making mistakes that July can learn and grow.

"Your storyteller is a woman possessed of a forthright tongue and little ink. Waxing upon the nature of trees when all know they are green and lush upon this island... is neither prudent nor my fancy. Let me confess this without delay so you might consider whether my tale is one in which you can find interest. If not, then be on your way."

MEMORABLE MOMENT One eventful evening sees July brazenly use dirty bed linen as the tablecloth at a high society dinner party and later attempt to steal the leftover wine, daringly from right under her master's nose.

ELEANOR OLIPHANT

HER STORY Eleanor Oliphant is a finance clerk struggling to deal with demons from her past in Gail Honeyman's award-winning debut novel *Eleanor Oliphant is Completely Fine*. We first meet her as a socially awkward loner, completely oblivious of her appearance and the butt of her co-workers' jokes, but she convinces herself that she is fine. According to Eleanor, people always let you down and having no friends is preferable, so she spends her weekends alone, drinking too much vodka. Gradually, the reader starts to uncover the clues that hint at the sad reasons behind Eleanor's unusual and self-destructive behavior, as we hear about the weekly phone calls from her abusive mother, a terrible house fire in her youth that has left her scarred, and years spent moving between different foster homes.

A couple of incidents propel Eleanor's lonely existence into new territory. First, she becomes infatuated with a singer, Johnnie Lomond, and convinces herself from afar that he is "the one" for her. Simultaneously, a friendship develops with her co-worker Raymond Gibbons. Raymond patiently strives to support Eleanor through social situations but Eleanor reaches a moment of crisis when she discovers that her fantasy Johnnie and the real Johnnie are very different people. This sudden shock of realization is accompanied by agonizing memories of past broken and abusive relationships and she spirals into total mental and physical breakdown. With Raymond's support, however, Eleanor is eventually able to return to work as a more balanced person and she welcomes his faithful friendship.

STRENGTHS Eleanor is incredibly brave. She has endured many damaging relationships in her past: a manipulative mother, countless foster families who rejected her, a physically abusive boyfriend, and bullying colleagues. It is no wonder she pushes people away and lives a solitary existence. So when challenged to disclose her demons and talk about her past, it takes immense courage and trust to open up to a therapist and to Raymond, and to allow the process of healing to begin.

A LITTLE DEEPER Eleanor's story is painful for us to hear. It is evident that her lifestyle is damaging and eccentric and when we watch her pursue a fantasy relationship with Johnnie and risk the blossoming true friendship with Raymond, we want to snap her out of her reverie! The reader cannot but be naturally drawn to Eleanor, empathizing with her current sorry state and her distressing past torments. We all want the best for her and cheer her on through her recovery. It is her success in conquering her demons that unquestionably makes her our heroine.

"If someone asks you how you are, you are meant to say FINE. You are not meant to say that you cried yourself to sleep last night because you hadn't spoken to another person for two consecutive days. FINE is what you say."

MEMORABLE MOMENT In an attempt to conform to fashion and attract the attention of her idol, Johnnie, Eleanor seeks out a personal shopper in a local department store and is persuaded to buy a totally unsuitable outfit, completely beyond both her budget and her comfort zone! When directed to the Bobbi Brown beauty counter for a makeover, she causes amusement by naively asking to speak to Bobbi herself. Eleanor is disillusioned by the entire experience.

KATNISS EVERDEEN

HER STORY In Suzanne Collins' trilogy *The Hunger Games*, Katniss Everdeen hails from District 12 in the fantasy nation of Panem. Each year, a barbaric contest sees two children from each of twelve districts fight to the death in an arena where the environment is fully manipulated by "Gamemakers." The Games are presented as a gruesome but entertaining sort of reality TV show, but in fact they exist to demonstrate the power and authority of President Snow's violent, dictatorial regime. When her younger sister is picked as "tribute" for the next Hunger Games, Katniss volunteers herself in her place. Her fight for survival is against the odds, besides which the rules state there can only be one victor. By careful manipulation of the rules, Katniss successfully saves both herself and fellow tribute Peeta Mellark and they both return home. A love triangle ensues between Katniss, Peeta, and Katniss' close childhood companion Gale Hawthorne.

However, Katniss' radical nonconformism sparks notions of mutiny among the tyrannized citizens of Panem, and President Snow feels increasingly threatened by the spread of her influence. Katniss and Peeta find themselves thrown into the arena again for a further Hunger Games, in which Katniss must find more ways to break the rules to save them a second time. All bets are off now and Katniss embodies The Mockingjay, symbol of The Rebellion, the developing underground movement intent on inciting a full revolution to end the Snow regime.

STRENGTHS Katniss is fully aware of her capabilities and shortcomings and focuses on employing her natural skills to fight, protect the people she cares about, and survive. Her moral compass is strong: she is inescapably drawn to helping and defending the vulnerable, even when it puts her in extreme danger.

A LITTLE DEEPER Katniss gains strength from her desire to protect those she loves; loyalty is crucial to her. But when shielding friends and family comes into conflict with defending the vulnerable, she is plagued by doubts, uncertain of the direction she should take. Her alliance with young Rue in the first Games is instinctive, yet it forces Katniss to make her first direct kill of another tribute. Much later, Katniss is conscious that inciting revolution as The Mockingjay could

benefit vulnerable citizens right across Panem if The Rebellion is successful. However, she is torn because open warfare would threaten the safety of her mother, sister, Peeta, and Gale.

"At some point, you have to stop running and turn around and face whoever wants you dead. The hard thing is finding the courage to do it."

MEMORABLE MOMENT Just before the second Hunger Games begin, the tributes are interviewed live on television. As these draw to a close, Katniss motivates all 24 tributes to hold hands in "the first public show of unity among the Districts since the Dark Days." This is a truly powerful moment as the first rumbles of rebellion begin.

HERMIONE GRANGER

HER STORY Hermione Granger is a witch and one of three main protagonists in J. K. Rowling's highly acclaimed *Harry Potter* series. Together with her friends Harry Potter and Ron Weasley, she attends Hogwarts School of Witchcraft and Wizardry, where they learn every aspect of magic and enjoy the usual student antics. Hermione is a keen academic and spends considerable time in the school library, completing her own and her friends' homework to the highest standard, as well as widening her knowledge from extra research and reading. In her third year at the school, she even uses a time turner to stretch her day and fit in extra school subjects! However, the trio frequently find themselves caught up in extracurricular adventures, which are alarmingly life-threatening. In her time, she is attacked by a basilisk, and faces up to such dangers as trolls, werewolves, dementors, and a dragon, not to mention being tortured by a dark witch.

Throughout the friends' younger years at school, the evil wizard Lord Voldemort is slowly returning to power and influence, advancing the threat and violence of dark magic among his followers, the death-eaters. As it becomes evident that Harry Potter must be the one finally to defeat Voldemort, Hermione proves herself an unwavering source of support and knowledge to Harry through the extreme challenges he must face alone, as well as a courageous soldier in the final battle of good versus evil.

STRENGTHS Hermione is naturally talented as a witch, highly intelligent, ambitious, and dedicated to extending her knowledge. Confident in her own abilities, she does however also possess an innate sensitivity and empathy toward others. She is loyal to the last.

"Me! Books! And cleverness! There are more important things—friendship and bravery..."

A LITTLE DEEPER Hermione certainly has a strong personality. She may come across as self-assured, but she faces familiar teenage problems: bullying by her peers, a burning desire to champion the oppressed, and the fluttering excitement and bitter heartbreak of young love.

MEMORABLE MOMENT We first warm to Hermione when she lies to her teachers, telling them she had deliberately confronted a troll to show off her skills. She takes the blame to protect her friends. Despite her supreme intelligence and self-confidence, on another occasion she accidentally transforms herself into a cat—hardly a typical teenage experience!

our heroine is born

We all come from different backgrounds with our own unique upbringing. We have each faced significant events in our childhood days that have shaped our future. And I'm sure we could all name family members and close friends whose influence has helped to make us who we are today. So the first question that springs to mind is whether a stable and supportive family background is necessary to become a heroine.

"For during the twelve years of her life she had been governed by love alone."

Little Women

Certainly, many of our key heroines experience a trouble-free childhood within a nurturing family environment. Hermione Granger seems to be a much-loved daughter. Although her parents appear only briefly in the narrative, it is made clear that despite being "muggles" (from the non-magic community), they support Hermione, encourage her keen intellect, and approve of her ambitions. What a stark contrast to the neglect and disinterest Harry Potter himself experiences from his only relatives, the Dursleys, who make him sleep in the cupboard under the stairs. (And who can forget the gift of a single paper tissue he receives from them one Christmas!)

Katniss Everdeen and her sister Primrose also come from a loving household, raised and cherished by an attentive father. The girls learn good behavior and polite manners, and Katniss has been taught the basics of hunting. This love experienced in childhood shines through Katniss, motivating her actions and decisions along her journey and contributing to her ultimate victory in the Hunger Games.

Jane Austen's sparky heroine Elizabeth Bennet has had an equally loving and stable upbringing. Her parents desire the best for each of their five daughters, encouraging them in their interests and talents. Moreover, Mrs. Bennet seeks out

opportunities for the girls to better themselves by securing an "advantageous match." Even if Lizzy is frequently embarrassed by her mother's pushy and unsubtle approach, she does end up as mistress of Pemberley, a huge and wealthy estate. Jo March and her three sisters have also enjoyed a childhood of affluence, comfort, and affection and are greatly inspired by the good examples set to them by their caring mother and charitable father.

"Think only of the past as its remembrance gives you pleasure."

Pride and Prejudice

So does a less fortunate family situation or disjointed and challenging upbringing have a negative impact on our future and the potential to become a heroine? Our next two protagonists have had difficult early experiences.

Eleanor Oliphant certainly has to overcome the consequences of a truly damaging childhood. The scars from her youth, revealed to the reader only gradually as the story progresses, are both physical and psychological. Her mother's erratic, controlling, and critical personality rules Eleanor's every action and thought, while the impact of her years in poor foster care means Eleanor struggles to empathize or even interact with other people, and she recoils from closeness or attachment. However, she deserves her place as one of our heroines because she rises above her distressing background and begins to learn simply to cope with life.

July faces a truly tough start to life: like her mother, she is destined from birth to be enslaved on a Jamaican sugar plantation and spend her life in servitude. However, July grows to be cheekily daring in the way she challenges rather than

accepts her situation. She constantly looks to gain small victories over her mistress, even if this is just by keeping her waiting, telling her untruths, or stealing a button from her dress. She is a heroine who makes the best she can of a life that is not really her own.

Another favorite literary heroine who rises above a painful start in life is Charlotte Bronte's Jane Eyre. As an orphan, she is on the lowest rung of society's ladder, yet by the end of her story, we find the well-known statement: "Reader, I married him," as she finally weds her beloved, the wealthy Mr. Rochester. In Winston Graham's *Poldark* series about a poor Cornish mining community, Demelza Carne is an illiterate and ill-mannered young girl, from a poverty-stricken family ruled by an aggressive father. However, as landowner Ross Poldark's wife, she embraces the opportunities her improved status affords, learning to read and write, successfully helping to manage her husband's mining business and socializing with the upper classes of society.

We cannot choose or change our family circumstances and upbringing; that is shaped by others and by destiny. But we can make the best of our start in life, be it positive or negative, and rise to become our own heroine.

BE YOUR OWN HEROINE

- Be grateful for a loving and supportive family.
- Your past may be part of you but need not define you.
- Dare to dream!

heroines are loyal to those closest to them

Families come in all shapes and sizes, and can encompass stepparents and children, grandparents raising their grandchildren, adoption, fostering, and more besides. Some people create a family from friends where they don't have one of their own, but whatever form it takes, it is the constant love and reliable support of your own particular "family" that is desirable and significant. Whatever their family background, true heroines show kindness and consideration and are positive, loyal, and caring members of their family.

"Family devotion only goes so far for most people on reaping day. What I did was the radical thing."

The Hunger Games

Supporting and protecting her family is fundamental to Katniss Everdeen, and she is constantly looking out for her mother and her beloved sister, Primrose. Every day she takes risks, hunting beyond the fence or trading on the black market to provide food. By far her most remarkable and selfless action is bravely volunteering herself as "tribute" to save her young sister from almost certain death, a decision that throws Katniss into the Hunger Games but is one that she never questions or regrets. She pleads with her friend Gale to look out for her family when she cannot, but in fact, it is surely her promise to Primrose, that she will return safely to continue caring for her family, that motivates her desperate fight for survival.

This brings to mind the big-hearted Nancy, in Charles Dickens' *Oliver Twist*, who fiercely tries to protect Oliver, for whom she feels a strong maternal affection. By defying Bill Sikes, she successfully reunites Oliver with his family, although in doing so she pays the highest price—her life.

Katniss is truly a heroine to her family, prepared to sacrifice her own life for them, and it is heartbreakingly poignant that she is ultimately unable to save her sister. Unfortunately, a similar tragedy is experienced by Eleanor Oliphant. Even as a child, Eleanor always did her best to protect her sister, trying to direct her mother's negative attentions on to herself. But here, I believe, is the clever twist in the tale: it is only at the very end of the novel that the true extent of Eleanor's heroic actions is revealed to the reader as we discover she had desperately tried but failed to save her younger sister from a fatal house fire.

These of course are extreme examples of protecting your family. In our ordinary everyday lives, we are (hopefully) less likely to face life or death situations. Two of our other heroines, Hermione Granger and July, have different sacrifices to make to protect their families.

In *The Deathly Hallows*, Hermione fears for the safety of her parents and her drastic solution is to erase their memories and get them far away from danger. Of course, as she herself is also wiped from their memory, Hermione loses their support during the difficult quest she and her friends must face, but this is a sacrifice she is prepared to make to keep her family safe. How far would you be prepared to go for your family?

July's protection of her child is a more real-life situation and again takes the form of a personal sacrifice. She believes the only way to secure a bright future for her son is by leaving him on the doorstep of a white man, a church minister. July's hopes are realized, as her son is raised as part of the minister's family, receives a good education, and eventually takes up an apprenticeship in London. This is far better than anything July could have provided for him.

Elizabeth Bennet and Jo March don't have to face danger or make huge sacrifices in order to protect their families, but nevertheless we recognize them as supportive daughters and sisters. Lizzy walks miles, through the mud, to nurse her sister Jane back to health—most unladylike behavior for the time! Later, she does everything she can to support her parents when her younger sister's elopement causes the deepest worry and shame.

Sometimes we need to defend our family against criticism, even when we may secretly feel critical of them ourselves. Lizzy, who is often quick to complain about the behavior of her mother and her younger sisters to her sister Jane, still defends them vigorously from criticism leveled at them by people outside the family. She deflects all the disparaging comments made at times by Mr. Darcy and Caroline Bingley, and who can forget her heated confrontation with Lady Catherine de Bourgh:

"He [Mr. Darcy] is a gentleman;
I am a gentleman's daughter;
so far we are equal."

Pride and Prejudice

Jo March and her sisters provide wonderful support to their mother while their father is away in the war. They take on household chores and give up all luxuries to help ease money worries. Jo even gets all her hair cut off and sells it to raise funds! The March girls are equally aware of the need to bolster their mother emotionally, striving to make her proud by being thoughtful, generous, and kind. Jo acts as paid companion to a relative, even though she finds it less than enjoyable, and she constantly looks out for all her sisters, most especially shy little Beth.

These examples of family loyalty may seem more mundane, but they are just as inspirational.

BE YOUR OWN HEROINE
- Family comes first!
- Be thoughtful and alert, looking for small ways to help.
- Simple gestures of kindness will be appreciated, even if it's just making your mother a nice cup of tea!

a heroine needs friends—
in good times and in bad

Family is important, but what about the people we choose to be part of our lives? I'm sure we all enjoy rummaging through boxes of old pictures and scrolling through photos on our phones to be reminded of all the happy times and funny moments spent in the society of good friends. As we journey through different stages of our life, we gather a circle of companions through shared experience and interests, and these friendships can really contribute to being your own heroine.

"Life is worth living as long as there's a laugh in it."

Anne of Green Gables

Jo March and her sisters welcome their lonely young neighbor Laurie into their lives, and together they have all sorts of fun, from picnics, parties, and ice-skating on the lake to playing pranks and running races—what a delightful and wholesome childhood! Lizzy Bennet and her friend Charlotte Lucas attend balls together and love to dance and gossip with other young ladies of the locality. Laughter and happiness are good for the soul and who better to create opportunities for fun times than good friends? However, our truest friends are those who stick by us through the tougher times as well, offering advice and help when the smiles have faded. A heroine need not face everything alone.

"I'll stand by you, Jo, all the days of my life. Upon my word I will!"

Little Women

Laurie and Jo are kindred spirits when it comes to joking around and causing mischief, but their friendship also has considerable depth. Laurie is a young gentleman, always looking out for Jo to make sure she is safe by offering his

carriage or walking her home from town when it is late and dark. It is when crisis hits the March family that Jo relies heavily on Laurie. With Mr. March and their sister Beth both dangerously ill, the sisters must look after the house and nurse a very sick Beth. Laurie willingly helps in small practical ways, by delivering messages or fetching things, but above all he offers comfort to Jo when she is at her lowest and in despair. He is her steadfast support.

"Jo felt the unspoken sympathy, and... the sweet solace which affection administers to sorrow."

Little Women

Shared experiences are one of the ways in which we can make friends or deepen our existing friendships. L. M. Montgomery's *Anne of Green Gables* also includes a firm friendship, between orphan Anne Shirley and her "bosom friend" Diana Barry. These two considerably different personalities build a long-lasting friendship from sharing the many ups and downs of youth, and Diana is a source of great comfort for Anne when her father-figure Matthew dies.

Not everyone finds building friendships comes naturally to them. Katniss Everdeen and Eleanor Oliphant are both introverts who shy away from getting close to people. Katniss explains how a friendship with Gale grew slowly through a shared interest in hunting, as she gradually began to trust him and enjoy his company on trips beyond the fence. She often recalls happy memories of times spent with Gale as a hunting partner, to escape mentally from the life-threatening so-called "Games." Katniss gradually gathers a group of friends who support her on the journey from being the girl from District 12, her impoverished home, to becoming The Mockingjay, symbol of the rebellion against the tyrannical regime.

Ironically, it is lonely Eleanor Oliphant who is of special interest in this chapter on friends! When we first meet Eleanor, she is living a solitary life; her only social interaction is with colleagues at work and her weekends are spent alone, largely under the alcoholic influence of Glen's Vodka. Initially, she is suspicious when her colleague Raymond approaches her, and she is reluctant and unable to engage with him. Nevertheless, she eats lunch with him at work, and from this seemingly trivial choice, companionship slowly grows. Trust is established, and with Raymond's gentle encouragement Eleanor accompanies him first on a hospital visit to their elderly friend, then to meet Raymond's mother, and even to attend a party. These relatively ordinary experiences prove to be moments of light and happiness when Eleanor finds herself in a dark and lonely place.

"Sometimes you simply needed someone kind to sit with you while you dealt with things."

Eleanor Oliphant is Completely Fine

Raymond's support proves crucial to Eleanor's very survival when an emotional breakdown leaves her in a dangerous and undernourished state. It is Raymond who finds her drunk and bruised. He washes her, encourages her to eat, and keeps a close eye on her, actions which surely save her life. He remains steadfast and compassionate through the months of Eleanor's recovery, and beyond, to a more stable life. It's safe to say that Raymond's support has a huge impact on Eleanor, seeing her through her darkest times and triggering her conscious decision to break away from her harrowing past.

Our heroines are wonderful examples of how listening to and leaning on our friends when things get difficult will help us sail more calmly through the stormy seas of life. Like Raymond and Laurie, we should also be there for them when the going gets rough.

BE YOUR OWN HEROINE
- Friends are the family we choose for ourselves. Be there for them.
- Share the good times—though ice skating is not for everyone!
- And share the bad times—we need not face problems on our own.

heroines can survive disappointment in love

Ah, the affairs of the heart: the most complicated and personal of all our relationships! Each person's experience of love is their own, but I think it is safe to say that romantic relationships have the capacity to make us vulnerable by stirring our deepest and most intimate hopes and feelings. Perhaps vulnerability isn't a quality that would traditionally be associated with heroism, which begs the question, is romantic love helpful on our quest to become heroines, or a hindrance?

"It is not time or opportunity that is to determine intimacy;—it is disposition alone. Seven years would be insufficient to make some people acquainted with each other, and seven days are more than enough for others."

Sense and Sensibility

Let us first contemplate the sad truth that unlike our favorite Disney films or rom-com movies, not all affairs of the heart end in "happy ever after." Things can go wrong, causing hurt and disappointment when they do.

Of our leading ladies, it is surely July and Eleanor Oliphant who experience the most negative outcomes from romantic liaisons. July's opportunity for love occurs when she catches the eye of the new overseer, Robert Goodwin, who is ostensibly sympathetic to the newly-emancipated workers and servants on the plantation. Totally smitten, Robert fixes upon an artful plan to marry the plantation owner, Caroline, in order to conduct an open affair with July. To July's delight, she can finally triumph over her mistress, flaunting her new position by wearing nice dresses, helping Robert run the plantation, and giving birth to his daughter. She certainly fancies herself in love, yet her fantasy comes crashing down. Frustrated and depressed by the workers' resistance to his plans, Robert rapidly switches his focus to Caroline and harshly rejects July, even raising a machete to strike her. His final act of cruelty is to trick her into giving up her beloved daughter as he sails away to a new life in England with Caroline. July is left heartbroken, alone, and penniless, to face the loss of her home on the plantation and an unknown future.

Eleanor also experiences crushing disappointment in love. Her naïve fixation on a local singer, Johnnie Lomond, becomes all-consuming; she constantly ponders ways to catch his eye and initiate what she truly believes will be her perfect relationship. She experiments with different outfits and nail colors, researches him on the internet, stalks him on social media, and even turns up at his home. We can't help but feel apprehensive about the inevitable catastrophe that is looming, as we witness her obsession grow ever more self-destructive. We find ourselves wanting to shout "don't do it, Eleanor...!" Yet poor Eleanor is so fixated on meeting her soulmate, so desperate to find a man that her mother would approve of, that she is blind to the absurdity of what she is doing. When realization finally hits home and her dreams suddenly come tumbling down, Eleanor is thrown into such despair that she spirals into emotional breakdown.

"After all these weeks of delusion, I recognized, breathless, the pure, brutal truth of it... and then that familiar black, black mood came down fast."

Eleanor Oliphant is Completely Fine

The devastation experienced by July and Eleanor is heart-wrenching for us to witness. They have opened their hearts to love and vulnerability, only to have their hopes and dreams smashed to pieces. This also brings to mind Marianne Dashwood in *Sense and Sensibility*, who feels an all-encompassing passion for Mr. Willoughby. Marianne is cruelly spurned, when fear of scandal and Willoughby's need for a wealthier wife brings their whirlwind romance to an abrupt end. The utter despair Marianne suffers as a result leads to severe illness. July, Eleanor, and Marianne all become victims to love, and their painful stories furnish us with a strong case against romantic love.

> "But why must I dwell upon sorrow? July's story will have only the happiest of endings."

The Long Song

However, Eleanor and July still have every right to their title of heroine. Their romantic encounters undeniably cause them serious harm, and yet with the support of friends and family, they both battle to recover and heal, ending up stronger than before. July eventually finds a contented and comfortable life with her son's family and maintains her sassy, positive outlook as she wrangles with her son to write down her life story exactly as she wants it told. And alongside Raymond's life-saving support, it is Eleanor's own determination to heal her emotional scars from years of abuse and loneliness that puts her on the road to recovery. During her convalescence, Marianne comes to appreciate Colonel Brandon's loving devotion and his offer of a steady and happy future. Yes, they have all had their heart broken, but they bounce back stronger. For me, July, Eleanor, and Marianne are true heroines and their resilience is an inspiration.

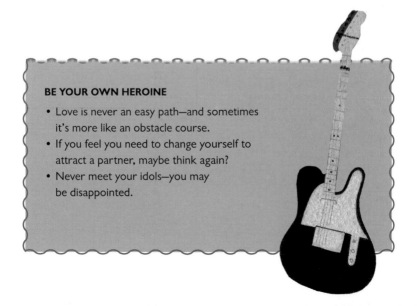

BE YOUR OWN HEROINE

- Love is never an easy path—and sometimes it's more like an obstacle course.
- If you feel you need to change yourself to attract a partner, maybe think again?
- Never meet your idols—you may be disappointed.

heroines don't
have to be alone

It may take a while, and there may be a few false starts (and painful stops), but happy endings do exist. Being a heroine certainly doesn't exclude you from finding happiness in love, so let's turn to more positive romantic adventures and explore the heroines who are lucky enough to have found their life partner.

"You don't need scores of suitors. You need only one... if he's the right one."

Little Women

Hermione's romance with Ron blossoms from an innocent and long-standing friendship that is not without its ups and downs. They are poles apart in their approach to schoolwork and petty squabbles arise frequently on such matters as The Society for the Protection of Elfish Welfare (SPEW), or the aggression shown by Hermione's cat Crookshanks toward Scabbers, Ron's pet rat. They also experience moments of jealousy over short-lived relationships with other partners. Tempers flare during the quest to hunt the horcruxes in *The Deathly Hallows*, and their relationship seems broken. Eventually, however, they acknowledge their mutual attraction and we leave them, years later, as a happily married couple with a family, despite (my favorite of her perceptive quips) Hermione's accusation that Ron has the emotional range of a teaspoon.

Katniss' complex relationship with Peeta is initially based on a façade: they portray themselves as lovers as a marketing ploy, to gain supporters and sponsorship for the Hunger Games. Out of the public eye, Katniss' feelings for Peeta are confused by her attraction to Gale, a rival for her love, and she is unsure where her heart truly lies. However, Katniss shares a strong and unique bond with Peeta, forged through mutual support as they desperately battle to

survive the awful ordeal that is the Games and then to heal from the resulting trauma. Katniss and Gale are firm friends, but it is Peeta's constant love and care that she eventually chooses. Her one desire has always been to return home and lead a peaceful, family-focused life.

> "...the idea of actually losing Peeta hit me again and I realized how much I don't want him to die... It's him. I do not want to lose the boy with the bread."

The Hunger Games

Unlike Hermione and Katniss, a young Demelza Carne weds Ross Poldark early in their relationship and their friendship develops later, as a married couple. Despite the many trials and challenges they face over the years, a wealth of shared experience only helps to strengthen the bond between them. Even danger and threats cannot destroy their love and loyalty to each other above all else.

First impressions between Lizzy Bennet and Mr. Darcy are the opposite of amorous—after all, no-one likes to be described as "tolerable!" Love only blossoms when mutual respect has been established, they have learned from each other, and they appreciate each other's true character. Lizzy realizes her initial judgment was prejudiced, while Darcy recognizes that his pride led him to make some blunders:

> "I cannot fix on the hour, or the spot, or the look, or the words, which laid the foundation. It was too long ago. I was in the middle before I knew that I had begun."

Pride and Prejudice

Lizzy and Darcy's hate-turns-to-love relationship is one of the most acclaimed in literature and has inspired many a love story since. Who can forget the brilliant

Bridget Jones? She grows to love her own Mr. Mark Darcy in much the same way, despite an early encounter with him in a ghastly Christmas sweater.

We have seen how shared experience, matching goals, friendship, and respect are the solid foundations of these heroines' successful love lives. (And it's noticeable that all of these things are missing from July's rushed and pressurized relationship with Robert, and from Eleanor's one-sided passion for Johnnie Lomond.) Each heroine and her chosen hero come to love and respect each other for who they really are, based on honesty and a complete lack of pretense. Therein lies our answer: romantic love that is based on truth and understanding can strengthen us on our quest to be our own heroine.

Before we move on, we have to consider Jo March in our research on love. If we agree with this conclusion, then surely Jo and Laurie would be a match made in heaven? Their firm friendship is built on shared interests and experiences, as well as the necessary fondness and respect for each other—surely a strong basis for a happy-ever-after ending, not to mention that Laurie is a rather good-looking young gentleman. Yet when Laurie does show interest in pursuing a romantic relationship, Jo rejects him. Instead, she exerts her independence by deciding to explore the wider world and expand her knowledge. This choice eventually leads her to a more suitable partner and a happy marriage, and although Professor Bhaer is quite a few years older than her, and not traditionally handsome, he certainly catches Jo's eye. Jo does not bow to expectation or pressure and only marries when it feels completely right for her.

BE YOUR OWN HEROINE
- The right match can inspire us to greater things.
- Never let yourself be persuaded into something that does not feel right.
- Remember you don't always need a partner to be a heroine.

heroines know how to stand up for themselves

Bullying is a sad fact of life, and it is unfortunately something that many of us experience, so it is hardly surprising that it also blights the lives of some of our literary heroines. They face a stressful, emotional trial as they seek to deal with tormentors without losing their sense of self, so what can we learn from them?

"I am not to be intimidated."

Pride and Prejudice

We know that bullies love to feel the power and control of belittling their victims and will express this through action. In *The Hunger Games*, it is the so-called "career tributes" who are the persecutors, flaunting their strength and brutality to exert power over the other "tributes." By forming a gang, the careers take control of food and weapons, hunting down vulnerable, lone-ranging tributes. Katniss is a clear target but is careful to avoid confrontation, knowing that she cannot match their mightier combat capabilities.

The most threatening bully on the Jamaican plantation is the original overseer, Tam Dewar, who asserts his position of control through physical acts of violence, designed to instill fear. He delights in beating and whipping as "punishment," while July herself is the product of his recurrent sexual abuse of her mother, Kitty. When the plantation owner commits suicide, Tam Dewar even goes so far as to pin this on Nimrod, a freed slave, as murder. As Nimrod and July stand trembling and pleading before him, he heartlessly shoots and kills Nimrod. He really is a nasty piece of work!

> "Although they may not be felt like a fist or a whip, words have a power that can nevertheless cower even the largest man to gibbering tears."

The Long Song

Some bullies dominate their victims through the power of words. Young Eleanor Oliphant is verbally abused by her mother to such an extent that she is engrained in Eleanor's subconscious. Her disembodied voice controls, derides, and influences Eleanor's poor choices. It is remarkable how we, the readers, are equally convinced of the reality of Eleanor's regular phone conversations with her mother.

Meanwhile in our wizarding world, Hermione is upset by Draco Malfoy's disdainful taunt of "mudblood." It is made abundantly clear that this is an extremely insulting term for those from non-magical parentage. Malfoy prides himself in his pureblood wizard family heritage and deems himself superior as a result.

Our earliest intimidator is Lady Catherine de Bourgh, Mr. Darcy's aunt in *Pride and Prejudice*. She attempts to establish dominance over Lizzy Bennet and frighten her into submission to prevent her potential marriage to Darcy. Convinced of the superiority of her own status, Lady Catherine confronts Lizzy in a purposefully degrading manner, listing reasons why Lizzy is not good enough for her nephew, and trying to extract from Lizzy a promise to refuse any proposal from Mr. Darcy.

Our heroines face bullies who intend to hurt them, whether physically or verbally, but each of them stands up for herself and fights back, retaining a sense of pride and thwarting the oppressor's attempts to gain control.

Katniss will not countenance becoming an ally of the careers in either of the Hunger Games; in fact, she is horrified when she misunderstands why Peeta has joined their gang. Despite their superior strength, Katniss outwits the careers with a combination of skill and intelligence. By climbing high into the trees, she places herself out of reach of any dangerous hand-to-hand combat and drops a nest of viciously poisonous mutant wasps on the gang. (I almost feel sorry for them...!) Even in her dangerous situation, July refuses to bow to pressure and clings to the truth, protesting Nimrod's innocence to the very end. Meanwhile, the pendulum finally swings in Eleanor Oliphant's favor when she stands up to her mother and tells her she is cutting off all future contact. This highly significant moment of separation allows Eleanor to progress on her journey toward healing and trust.

" 'Goodbye, Mummy,' I said. The last word. My voice was firm, measured, certain. I wasn't sad. I was sure."

Eleanor Oliphant is Completely Fine

Lizzy Bennet stands tall and shows no sign of being intimidated by Lady Catherine's insulting words. Rather than cowering at the slights on both her and her family, she argues back strongly, refusing to be bullied into submission, even though at this point she has no expectation of a proposal from Darcy.

BE YOUR OWN HEROINE
- Stay strong and true to yourself and your beliefs.
- See bullies for the cowards that they really are.
- Retaliating with a nest of mutant wasps may be tempting and satisfying— but is not advisable!

heroines learn to love themselves

Having considered relationships and interactions with other people on our journey to becoming a true heroine, what about our relationship with ourself?

When we look in the mirror, there are almost certainly bits of our physical appearance that make us self-conscious and which we wish we could change. We may think we are too tall or too short, that we possess a protruding nose, or—the perennial problem—that we have a few extra pounds to lose after Christmas! And we fear our outward appearance is going to prejudice the opinions of others, even before they've got to know us. We may feel pressure to conform to what we think is the norm, but true heroines learn to love themselves as they are: they accept all their foibles and imperfections and they trust that other people will also look beneath the outer shell and uncover their real character.

"She had tried to steer me towards vertiginous heels again—why are these people so incredibly keen on crippling their female customers?"

Eleanor Oliphant is Completely Fine

Social media can be a blessing, but it regularly hits the headlines as the culprit for a growing obsession with our looks, as we compare ourselves with celebrities or online influencers, and find ourselves wanting. Photoshopping is also to blame: now that it is all too easy to erase perceived imperfections digitally, the manipulated images of other people we see online give us an unrealistic idea of what we should look like and how our life should be. It is becoming sadly common for all of this to cause depression and a sense of inadequacy.

Turning to two of our heroines for inspiration, I don't believe either July or Hermione are ashamed of their looks, nor are they concerned if others judge them. On the contrary, they are confident in themselves and their abilities.

In the years before and even after the abolishment of slavery, racism was an accepted part of daily life in Jamaica, and skin color determined your status: the lighter your skin tone, the more chance you had for progression in society and an increase in wealth. July's dark black skin is therefore regarded as a misfortune and she is viewed as one of the lowest in society. She tries to promote her mixed-race status—her mother was black, her father white—but July is disappointed when she is considered too dark to attend social gatherings in town. Yet she is neither ashamed of her skin color, nor accepting of her low status; she does not let it hold her back as she continually seeks ways to progress and find fulfillment. After a chance meeting with her long-lost son, she embraces her final years as a respectable lady in a comfortable home, becoming a successful published writer and sharing her story with the world.

In her early years at Hogwarts, Hermione is not considered pretty; she is teased for her bushy hair and large teeth, and her posture is compromised by carrying around a heavy bagful of books. At the Halloween feast in her first year, we learn that she has hidden away in tears after overhearing Ron describe her as a "nightmare," an unkind criticism of her "showing off" in Charms. Yet as she grows up, the judgments of fellow students do not distract Hermione from what she deems important. She certainly never fusses or complains about her looks. Her metamorphosis comes at the Yule Ball in her fourth year at school, when she straightens her hair and wears a stunning dress, causing Ron and Harry suddenly to notice Hermione's physical charms! (Or, in Ron's case, to notice she is in fact... a girl!) But the following day, she returns to her usual, "comfortable" self. Hermione has invested in pursuing knowledge and skills above image.

On the surface, it may seem that Eleanor has a similarly confident attitude toward her outward appearance, but she has scars, both physical and mental, from her early life experiences. Her burned skin, caused by the house fire, is painful and frequently attracts stares. The mental legacy of her mother's abuse causes Eleanor to retreat from people into a lonely world of repetitive routine and unhappiness. Eleanor therefore chooses clothes, shoes, and a haircut all seemingly based on practicality rather than fashion. She wears her hair long and unstyled and sticks with flat, clumsy shoes because they are comfortable. Gloves hide the scars on her hands but are mocked by her co-workers. She tells the reader that stares don't get her down and that she doesn't care what people think about her dress sense, but is there a more negative motivation behind her style choices? Is she putting up a defensive barrier to prevent any friendly but unwelcome overtures? Despite her apparent lack of interest in her appearance, the first thing she does to try and attract Johnnie's attention is to alter how she looks, in an attempt to conform to social norms.

Of course there are literary heroines who are more aware of their image, and as few of us feel sufficiently self-confident to brush aside the opinions of friends and colleagues on this subject, perhaps we can relate to their concerns.

"I'm pore, I'm black, I may be ugly and can't cook, a voice say to everything listening. But I'm here."

The Color Purple

Celie in *The Color Purple*, by Alice Walker, is ashamed of her appearance, following repeated abuse in her youth and being told she is ugly. She shrinks into silence, as well as passive acquiescence to the abusive men in her life, confiding only in God. It is only when Celie's role model, Shug Avery, teaches Celie to fight back and feel empowered that she discovers her own voice and a feeling of self-worth. She begins to stand up for herself and works to secure a more contented and fulfilling life.

Our heroines rise above the insults and scorn of others, focusing instead on their strengths and ambitions to achieve great things. Perhaps we should follow their lead, and pay more attention to our inner selves and our aspirations in life.

BE YOUR OWN HEROINE

- Celebrate your appearance, imperfections and all.
- Don't judge a book by its cover.
- Take social media images with a pinch of salt...

heroines aren't perfect

We've looked at how heroines feel about their physical appearance, but there may also be aspects of our temperament that we don't like—impatience, an introvert nature, or (as in my case!) a tendency to talk too much. What should we do if we detect in ourselves some less desirable character traits? Although these flaws will undoubtedly be deep-seated, a true heroine can nevertheless endeavor to change any that have a negative impact on other people.

"Poor Jo tried desperately to be good, but her bosom enemy was always ready to flame up and defeat her."

Little Women

Jo March is ashamed of those occasions when she gives way to the anger that can overwhelm her, and she recognizes that it adversely affects her relationships. When Amy makes the rash decision (swiftly regretted) to burn Jo's beloved notebook full of jottings for her novel, Jo is thrown into a fit of rage that cannot be assuaged by Amy's sincere, heartfelt apologies. Jo seethes and sulks for days, lashing out verbally and rejecting all attempts at reconciliation. It is only when Amy's life is endangered by falling into a frozen lake that Jo is shocked out of her fury into profound remorse. Ashamed at her lack of self-control and with the support of her mother and fervent prayers to God, she consciously strives to overcome her tendency to anger. This is no easy task for Jo, but she recognizes the negative effects her anger has on others and tries hard to change her nature.

Lizzy Bennet is similarly embarrassed by her first, misjudged opinions of Darcy and Wickham. She prided herself on her judgment of character, believing Darcy to be arrogant and haughty and Wickham an honest and charming gentleman, poorly treated by Darcy, but events were to prove her first impressions very wrong. Lizzy "grew absolutely ashamed of herself. Of neither Darcy nor Wickham could she think without feeling she had been blind, partial, prejudiced, absurd."

BE YOUR OWN HEROINE

- Speak angrily in haste, repent at leisure.
- We all have faults, but that doesn't mean we can't try and overcome them.
- First impressions aren't always accurate.

heroines are proud of where they come from

Unfortunately, even in our more enlightened and liberal twenty-first-century society, we can still face unfair and narrow-minded judgments, based on where we live and our supposed "status" in society. A strong accent in our speech can of course betray the geographical location of our upbringing and this could contribute to a prejudiced first impression, regardless of what we are saying. True heroines will be proud of their background and able to overcome any bias to prove themselves.

"District 12: Where you can starve to death in safety."

The Hunger Games

Within the fantasy society of *The Hunger Games*, District 12 is considered the lowliest of districts, yet Katniss is very proud of her origins. In fact, she considers the down-to-earth nature of District 12 inhabitants, born out of the daily grind of poverty and hunger, a superior quality to the decadence, indulgence, and pretense that are the foundations of society in the higher districts and the Capitol. And as we know, from this humble background, Katniss eventually rises to become the most renowned person in Panem.

In the magical community of *Harry Potter*, witches and wizards of muggle parentage face prejudice from a sector of arrogant purebloods. We have already heard how the bully Draco Malfoy labels Hermione with the derogatory term "mudblood." This behavior seems to have been influenced by his father Lucius, who makes it clear that he despises Ron's father, Mr. Weasley, for his curiosity about the everyday items used by muggles (electric fires, paper money, plugs, and screwdrivers—all truly fascinating artefacts to a wizard!). But our heroine Hermione proves them all wrong, showing beyond all doubt that muggle-born witches and wizards are capable of excelling in the magical world. Hermione is

top of the class, outstanding in both skills and knowledge and is widely acknowledged as the "cleverest witch of her age."

In the early-nineteenth-century setting of *Pride and Prejudice*, the Bennet family's social status continually haunts Lizzy as the story unfolds. Caroline Bingley scorns Lizzy and her family for their perceived lesser rank and respectability in comparison with her own circle, which is particularly ironic since Austen makes it clear that the Bingley family's wealth originates from success in trade. The Bennets' cousin Mr. Collins is a personal favorite of mine among Austen's comic characters. He flaunts a moral high ground from his position as a clergyman, as well as a supposed social superiority derived from his acquaintance with the eminent Lady Catherine de Bourgh. And we cannot forget that an initially haughty and misguided Mr. Darcy slights Lizzy and her family, looking down on them from his status of rich landowner "with ten thousand a year." In his first proposal to Lizzy, he makes the mistake of asking her, "Could you expect me to rejoice in the inferiority of your connections?—to congratulate myself on the hope of relations, whose condition in life is so decidedly beneath my own?" But despite these put-downs, our heroine Lizzy considers herself his equal and does not change her aspirations.

It is challenging to be true to who you are in the face of derision and mockery. It can be tempting to take the easier way out and back down from confrontation, or pretend to be from a different background or place, but sooner or later we need to accept who we are and where we have come from. Perhaps we can take courage from a few other heroines who experience moments of hesitation.

"You can transmute love, ignore it, muddle it, but you can never pull it out of you."

A Room with a View

In E. M. Forster's novel *A Room with a View*, Lucy Honeychurch faces a realistic and problematic choice: to marry for love or marry for money? (Not a bad choice to have, if truth be told!) Lucy is temporarily swayed by the strong temptation to marry Cecil, a man from the higher echelons of society, to better herself and to gain financial security. Does she follow her head or her heart? Her short-lived engagement to Cecil brings to the fore his arrogant disdain for Lucy's fellow townsfolk and ultimately leads to her decision to marry for love, despite the lower social status of her chosen partner.

Anne Elliot in Jane Austen's *Persuasion* faces a similar predicament. As a young woman, she was persuaded by family to end her engagement to a lieutenant in the Royal Navy because of his lower social status and uncertain prospects. It is a more mature and self-confident Anne who has the strength to trust her instincts and follow her heart, so that the couple can be reunited.

Even Katniss experiences moments of doubt. Following their victory at the first Hunger Games, Katniss and Peeta are obliged to tour the other districts to make speeches to the citizens. They are given a prescribed text to deliver and forced to act in a way that promotes President Snow and the Games. Katniss tries to do as she is told in the belief that it will result in Snow leaving her and her family alone, to live a quiet life. However, she is truly troubled by the pretense and it causes her to waver. She feels the anguish of the bereaved families of fallen tributes and is further moved by hearing a few brave citizens speak out against the regime, despite the severe punishment that results.

Changing our relationship with ourselves can be a real challenge. Embracing an element of our physical appearance we are ashamed of takes courage, while overcoming insecurity about how others perceive our social standing takes confidence. It is never easy to maintain a positive view of ourselves when it is tested by other people's judgments. But like our literary paradigms, if we can be kind and true to ourselves, as well as to others, we are well on the way to becoming our own heroine.

BE YOUR OWN HEROINE

- A combination of head and heart makes for wise decisions.
- Remember: don't judge a book by its cover... or its price.
- You can be as great as the next person.

heroines bend the rules when necessary

Your first experience of community "rules" and regulations will probably have been at school. Were you like me, doing everything you could to avoid a telling-off or a dreaded letter home to your parents? Or perhaps you were more laid back, and less worried by the threat of detention or being sent to the principal?

For a society to work successfully, a few rules are essential. Without them, the world would be an anarchic and frightening place to live in—imagine driving a car without road signs, traffic lights, or speed limits! Most of us are lucky enough to live in a benevolent democracy where the rules are agreed by majority decisions. In order to fit in, we must abide by these guidelines, even when we don't necessarily agree with them wholeheartedly. But what if we recognize danger or evil in authority? Should a heroine always stick to the rules?

"I really can't think about kissing when I've got a rebellion to incite."

Catching Fire (The Hunger Games)

Katniss immediately springs to mind because deliberate non-compliance is integral to her character; she refuses to conform either to the rules or to the gamemakers' expectations of her. In the first Games, she follows her instincts and her conscience by choosing not to hunt down other tributes, preferring instead to wander far away to the edges of the arena. She places flowers on her friend and fallen tribute Rue's body out of respect and she devises the double suicide plan, eating poison berries simultaneously with Peeta. Her intention is to highlight the immorality of the Games. However, her courage spurs others to stand up to the bullying authority of Snow's administration and eventually sparks the flame of a widespread rebellion. In the second Hunger Games, she successfully inspires a united front from all the tributes, who ultimately destroy

the dome over the arena. Eventually, she openly joins the rebellion and becomes its symbol, The Mockingjay. Katniss is certainly no law-abiding citizen, but the goal of her insubordination is to challenge a corrupt society, led by a cruel and feared dictator. It successfully leads to a thorough shake-up of that society's regulations and norms.

Hermione begins her school life as a stickler for following the rules, but adapts as she matures, when her innate moral compass convinces her that breaking rules will sometimes be the optimal way forward. She begins to recognize that she must trust her instincts and act courageously in order to tackle cruelty and evil. In *The Order of the Phoenix*, she improvises some outright lies to the sadistic Professor Umbridge to trick her into entering the Forbidden Forest. Hermione's successful deception leads Umbridge to be captured by angry centaurs, which in turn allows Harry and his friends to mount a rescue mission to the Ministry of Magic. In *The Deathly Hallows*, the famous trio of Hermione, Harry, and Ron drop out of society completely and go on the run, keeping under cover in order to battle the rise of Lord Voldemort and the death eaters. Our heroine does not hesitate to become a rebel in times of need, in the face of injustice and terrifying authority.

Compared with our everyday lives, these are extreme, somewhat surreal examples of rule-breaking and rebellion. We are unlikely to find ourselves in a life-threatening situation similar to either Katniss or Hermione, but they can still inspire us with their brave choices. They are each guided by a strong moral compass. When faced with the injustice of those in power hurting the innocent, rather than taking the easier route of passive acquiescence, they both make a stand and challenge authority, despite the threat of personal danger.

"Don't try to make me grow up before my time..."
Little Women

Katniss and Hermione are breaking unjust laws with their rebellious behavior, but perhaps more relatable for us are the heroines, equally audacious, who stand up to the restrictive "rules" and traditional expectations of society in their era. Elizabeth Bennet and Jo March frequently challenge the social norms and behave in a manner contrary to that which is expected of them. Both these young ladies are open and outspoken, and do not hold back from speaking their minds, at a time when women were supposed to remain reticent and polite in tone. Both women gallivant around the countryside, getting their dresses torn and muddy—terribly inappropriate behavior for young women of their class at the time. Amy is horrified by Jo's behavior when they are making social calls on friends and relations in the neighborhood, finding both her demeanor and her conversation extremely distasteful and embarrassing. And Lady Catherine de Bourgh can scarcely believe her ears when Lizzy has the nerve to answer back to her, countering Lady Catherine's opinion and demands with a strong defense of herself and her family.

Another fantasy heroine who defies social expectations is Éowyn in J. R. R. Tolkien's *The Lord of the Rings: The Return of the King*. Middle Earth standards dictate that women do not fight in combat. Yet Éowyn is so passionate to help in the fight against Sauron that she disguises herself as a man and sallies forth with the Riders of Rohan into The Battle of Pelennor Fields, where she takes down the terrifying King of the Ringwraiths.

So, what can we learn from the actions of our heroines? They each approach their situation in different ways but all of them stand up bravely for what they believe in and for themselves. They permit neither rules nor expectations to sway their moral stance and the desire to uphold truth and goodness.

BE YOUR OWN HEROINE
- Fight for what's right—stick to a strong moral code.
- Don't always follow the crowd.
- A bit of mud on your dress won't hurt and will wash out...

conclusion: heroines are brave

"I want to do something splendid... something heroic or wonderful... and I mean to astonish you all someday."

Jane Eyre

What a journey we have traveled in this, our exploration of true heroines! By looking at the words, actions, and stories of a few of our favorite characters, we have discovered some simple truths, which will hopefully give us food for thought and some inspiration for our own lives.

Our heroines were shaped by relationships with friends and family, and they were confident in themselves, in their abilities, and in their convictions about right and wrong, good and evil. They were prepared to flout the rules and society's norms and even to risk personal danger for the good of others. Truly, they are influential role models from whom we can learn so much. So how can we kick-start the journey to being our own heroine?

First, let's go back to basics. If you look up the term "heroine," the word that pops up most frequently is bravery. Our leading literary ladies originate from several historical eras, some from fantasy worlds and some from the real world. They are of different colors and cultures, their individual social standing and financial status is wide-ranging, and they all have particular desires, differing motives, and their own journeys. Yet they certainly all share one unquestionable attribute: bravery.

Hermione and Katniss show genuine courage by putting lives on the line—their own and sometimes those of loved ones—in order to bring down the corrupt and evil. It takes tough decisions, unceasing determination, and drastic actions, but they succeed.

Eleanor Oliphant had taken refuge in a lonely, routine-driven existence—and breaking habits is one of the most difficult things to achieve. In the course of the

novel, we see her bravely facing up to the past and putting it firmly behind her, symbolically demonstrated in the final conversation with her mother. Once she has said goodbye to her forever, we know that this is a turning point and she will move on toward a better, "completely fine" future.

"Small but courageous acts of defiance."

The Long Song

July's bravery can be seen simply in the way she lives her life as best she can: with resilience—surviving with a laugh those times when she is made a victim—with humor, and with a bit of cheeky insubordination. Through heartbreak and loss she fights on, making the best of it.

Jo March demonstrates her courage by believing in her talents, by refusing to let anything get in the way of what she wants and what she loves, and above all by being true to her strong personality. Despite setbacks, she pursues her own path until she reaches her goal.

"My courage always rises at every attempt to intimidate me."

Pride and Prejudice

Lizzy bravely sticks to her guns and doesn't allow parents, peers, or social superiors to influence her firmly-held opinions or her path in life. Defying convention, she won't be persuaded to marry for money or security but holds out for a marriage of love and respect. She finds all she ever wants in Mr. Darcy.

We are all shaped by different backgrounds, circumstances, likes and dislikes, hopes and dreams, obstacles and problems. But it doesn't matter, that's just life! Whoever we are and wherever we find ourselves, if we can bravely step out of our comfort zone and be courageous in our words and actions, then like our literary protagonists, we too will be well on our way to becoming our own heroine.

further reading

Louisa May Alcott:
Little Women (1868)
Good Wives (1869)
Little Men (1871)
Jo's Boys (1886)
Jane Austen:
Sense and Sensibility
(1811)
Pride and Prejudice
(1813)
Mansfield Park (1814)
Emma (1815)
Northanger Abbey (1817)
Persuasion (1817)
Charlotte Brontë, *Jane
Eyre* (1847)
Suzanne Collins:
The Hunger Games
(2008)
Catching Fire (2009)
Mockingjay (2010)

Charles Dickens, *Oliver
Twist* (1838)
Helen Fielding, *Bridget
Jones's Diary* (1996)
E. M. Forster, *A Room
with a View* (1908)
Winston Graham:
Ross Poldark (1945)
Demelza (1953)
Gail Honeyman, *Eleanor
Oliphant is Completely
Fine* (2017)
Andrea Levy:
Small Island (2004)
The Long Song (2010)
L. M. Montgomery,
Anne of Green Gables
(1908)
J. K. Rowling:
*Harry Potter and the
Philosopher's Stone*
(1997)

*Harry Potter and the
Chamber of Secrets*
(1998)
*Harry Potter and the
Prisoner of Azkaban*
(1999)
*Harry Potter and the
Goblet of Fire* (2000)
*Harry Potter and the
Order of the Phoenix*
(2003)
*Harry Potter and the
Half-Blood Prince* (2005)
*Harry Potter and the
Deathly Hallows* (2007)
J. R. R. Tolkien, *Lord of
the Rings* (1954)
Alice Walker, *The Color
Purple* (1982)

acknowledgments

Thank you to Ailsa for being such a fantastic sounding board when we needed
to bounce ideas back and forth about the best literary heroines to include.
Thanks go to our mum, Jane, for invaluable editing and proofreading. Also to
Abigail for some great feedback and constructive criticism throughout the writing
process. And I can't forget the talented Yelena for the wonderfully colorful
illustrations throughout our book—thank you!

index